MW00328513

THE REALITY TV PRODUCER AND DIRECTOR HANDBOOK

Donald Ian Bull

Intersection Productions, Inc.

STUDIO CITY, CALIFORNIA

Donald Bull/Intersection Productions
4307 Vantage Avenue
Studio City, CA, 91604
www.intersectionproductions.com

The Reality TV Producer and Director Handbook/ Donald Bull. -- 1st ed.
ISBN 978-1-948873-07-9

Donald Ian Bull has produced, directed and edited many reality TV shows over the past twenty years, including *The Real World, Road Rules, Bug Juice, Camp Jim, Wild Things, The Osbournes, Dr.90210, Beverly Hills Nannies, Project Runway* and more.

He also writes thrillers under the pen name Ian Bull. He is the author of *Liars in Love*, and *Reality Roadkill (A Love Story),* and the thriller series *The Quintana Adventures,* which includes *The Picture Kills* and *Six Passengers, Five Parachutes*. The third book, *Danger Room,* will be out soon.

He also writes nonfiction essays: *CaliforniaBull*, and *Water Markers: Essays on Swimming.*

Please write a review of this book! It will help me reach more readers! Email me at:

IanBullauthor@gmail.com

and I'll show you how.

You can find more writing and free downloads at:

IanBullAuthor.com

Dedicated to all the documentary shooters who know how to cover a scene with one camera.

CONTENTS

PREFACE

This is a compilation of ideas about what works well during the production of a reality based show, from one person's point of view.

After reading this, crew people new to reality TV will hopefully understand what goes into making a reality show -- but this is just one kind of reality show, and one way of producing that kind of show.

Experienced crew people will both agree and disagree with what's written here and we welcome feedback.

This is meant to be a broad overview, so certain ideas may work well on some reality TV shows and not on others.

This is also not complete -- this document will continue to be changed and updated as more ideas are added.

INTRODUCTION

THE ESSENTIAL DILEMMA: There is an ironic contradiction that takes place during the production of a reality show.

When things are good:

When the show is working well, less footage is being shot in the field. The production crew seems to get better stories with less work.

This means there is: less footage to injest and to dub...less footage to log and group clip in the edit bay...the story department watches less material...and finally...there is less footage in the edit bay.

Stories are easier to outline in the story department and easier for editors to put together.

The entire show is easier for everyone concerned and the overall show is cheaper and easier to produce.

When things are not working well:

When the show is not working well, the production crew is shooting too much footage and not getting enough story material. Why?

It could be the first week of production and everyone is still getting used to one another.

Maybe there isn't enough "story" material happening, so the crew is working extra hard shooting anything and everything that might work.

This may also happen because there is an attitude in TV that shooting is easy. Why fill just two cards when you can fill six? If two is good, six is better.

But six cards take three times longer to injest than two...three times longer for the assistant editors, and they create three times as much work for the story department and the editors.

Those six cards have tripled the overall cost and time of post-production -- although the cost in the field is just a few more cards.

Back in the home office, the post-production department ends up making specific story decisions to cut down on the huge volume of material.

The story department and the editors then make the final creative decisions about what's important, and what footage is left behind, and that ___takes the crew out of the creative process.___

Often on reality shows production crews feel their best material is not getting used.

There's a sense of frustration because no one knows whether what they're shooting will every end up in an episode...so shooting great material ends up feeling the same as mediocre material.

This, in turn, creates a gulf between the production and post-production crew. The production crews complain that the people in post missed the best stuff, while the people in post complain that the crews never followed the right stories.

So, what's the solution? ***Invest everyone on the crew in the story.***

If everyone on the crew and in post is always thinking about the story, they feel more invested in the work.

There is a misconception that on a reality show you just shoot everything that happens -- and then later it's turned into a story. That attitude creates too much footage and too much work for everyone.

On a reality TV show a good production crew already has an idea how each shot will be used, and for which story-line. They also know why other shots get left behind.

If everyone on the crew thinks this way, then the fun part of telling the story will be shared by everyone. ***Make sure everyone knows as much about the entire process.*** That way needless work will be avoided, and the work that is done will be used.

There's lots of reasons why footage gets ignored. If the crew knows what doesn't work, they can avoid needless work.

Also, if everyone on the crew stays conscious of the amount of material being shot, what is considered "good material" will become clear.

If you shoot everything and treat everything as important, then nothing is important. It's all the same. People will joke, "we shoot the paint drying."

SECTION ONE: *To Teach People Every Position.*

Every member of the crew contributes to the story. We want every crew member to understand every other crew member contribution.

This document is not meant to teach a camera shooter how to shoot, for example. Most reality TV shooters are already experienced professionals.

Instead, this document is designed so that you can read how the other people in other crew positions contribute to getting the story. That way you can streamline your own work to better match theirs.

Everyone wants their work to be used, and the best way to ensure that is to understand how your own work fits into the overall machine.

The worst feeling is to do great work that gets passed over or can't be used!

We hope that crew people will read their sections and give notes so we can make their jobs even more clear in future documents.

SECTION TWO: *To Help People with the "Tricks of the Trade."*

This is a long section about what works and what doesn't during production on a reality show. Hopefully it will help new crew people, and be starting point for discussion. That way we'll create better stories with less footage!

SECTION ONE:
THE VARIOUS
POSITIONS

THE PRODUCER

Ultimately, all creative and monetary decisions end up with the producer. The producer stays with the show from beginning to end, long before production begins, and long after post-production ends.

This means the overall vision for the series starts and ends with the producer. He hires directors, editors, shooters and audio people to help him realize that vision.

He works with the executive producers, the network that airs the show, the budgets, the day-to-day logistics of production. And then he still must deliver an interesting series with compelling stories that people want to watch.

It's the producer's show.

CAMERA SHOOTERS

There are several ideas to always keep in mind about any cameraperson: When the cameraperson is shooting, he/she is doing 50 things at once.

They are shooting a scene.

They are thinking about the shots they must get to make that scene work in the edit bay.

They are listening to the director on headset and incorporating his direction.

They are listening and judging some mix of audio coming out of the camera. Is it clear? Is it good?

They are thinking about which filter they are on, and the quality of the image.

They are doing a "dance" with their audio person.

If the shooter is also the DP, he is advising the shooters under him and thinking about the overall look of the show.

They also do all of this while seeing the world as a tiny black and white image in viewfinder.

This means that shooters tend to be very stressed.

IT STARTS WITH THE SHOOTER

"Getting the story" starts with the shooter. They must push the "record" button to roll camera. If that happens, something can be turned into a story. If they miss something, then there's no story.

COVERAGE

Getting "coverage" is the process of getting the basic shots an editor needs to edit a scene, while a scene is taking place.

It's hard for beginning camera shooters to understand what is needed in basic coverage...unless they've edited their own material together and seen what works and what doesn't work.

Experienced shooters have often produced, directed and edited, and they understand what works and what doesn't.

"Coverage" consists of establishing shots, wide shots, medium shots, close-ups, over-the shoulder shots, listening shots, cutaway shots...all captured the scene is taking place.

The cameraperson must work like crazy just to pop off the necessary shots before the scene changes or disappears. Sometimes, a crucial shot gets missed.

But a good shooter has tricks to condense all those coverage shots into a few great shots that can cover a scene.

Sometimes a wide shot can also double as a profile shot for a cast member who at the edge of the frame. You see that character speaking, and the rest of the room is seen and established in the background.

Experienced camera shooters also shoot plenty of reaction shots. They tell more about what's going on than the shot of the person speaking. The editor also uses them to shorten the scene.

These are just two tricks good "coverage" shooters use. An entire book can be written about how to get coverage. The best way to learn it is to find the good coverage shooters and ask them what works!

Listening and Anticipating

A good shooter is listening as much as he or she is shooting. If the cast is talking about wanting to leave, the shooter is already anticipating where he should stand in the hallway when people start to go.

Cast members have habits, and the shooter learns them. Who's in the bathroom first? Who's always out the door last? The shooter adapts to everyone's rhythms and is there for the story when it happens.

Getting More than Just Coverage

An experienced camera shooter will also do more than just capture the basic coverage shots -- they listen and seen to capture something else -- a moment, or a nuance, which they heighten with the right camera shot or angle.

This is because they are tuned into the scene and they are listening. They also know the cast member's life stories. They know if two cast members are fighting, or if two cast members have a blossoming romance.

The shooter is already anticipating the next story beat in each of those dramas. By talking with crew, everyone can also agree what those beats may be.

Providing the "Look" of the Show

Ultimately, the "look" of this show, and all documentary shows are the same -- a guy/gal with a camera on his or her shoulder gets a whole bunch of hand-held shots.

The challenge is to somehow make the look of the show transcend this basic limitation.

The Producer, the Director, and the Director of Photography are all working together to find ways to shoot coverage, interviews and B-roll in new and interesting ways so that each reality TV show has its own look.

Creative Responsibility

A lot of creative responsibility rests with the shooter. If everything is going well, it's clear to everyone what's worth shooting and what's not. It's also clear which "tricks" work.

But if there's a problem, it's very easy for a camera shooter to do what they want and just keep shooting.

This may be good -- at least the camera is rolling and a story is being recorded. If the shooter is experienced, he can be a lifesaver.

But if it happens too much, then the camera shooter is shooting his own version of the story -- which might not match with the other twenty people working on the show. This creates more footage and more story problems down the line.

THE SOUND PERSON/ AUDIO ENGINEER

There is a tendency to rank the cameraperson as higher than the audio person on the crew. After all, the camera is the more glorious job.

However, the audio engineer is of equal importance as the cameraperson...especially when it comes to STORY. You can tell what's going on in Jurassic Park even when the sound is off...but not on a reality show.

That's because even when a reality TV is at its most adventurous, it's first and foremost a show about personal relationships. For those stories you need audio as much as picture.

The audio engineer has a much different challenge than the cameraperson. His stress is not as constant as the cameraperson. His stress comes in short intense waves.

When you start shooting a scene, the audio engineer must make sure he's getting the audio he wants right away. He puts lavaliers on certain cast members, changes microphones, changes batteries -- it's big stress!

But then, things settle down. The audio engineer has headphones on that isolate him into his own world. He hears no director yelling at him, no one from the crew is asking him a question.

He's also not staring at a monitor. His line of vision is wide. He can make eye contact with people as they walk by. When someone is coming that will change his mixing strategy, he can anticipate.

He can see the whole picture better than the cameraperson, who's trapped staring at a black and white image on a viewfinder. He can also see the whole picture better than the director, who is hiding behind a bush nearby.

His job is still very complicated. Mixing three lavaliers and a boom microphone and then swapping BP90 batteries while dodging a one-eyed cameraman is HARD. But he has fewer outside distractions once he's working.

He's also the person who has the most direct contact with the cast members, day and night. Why? Because he must teach them the technical responsibilities of wearing a microphone. He straps them up, he changes their batteries. He raps with them. There's a little patter between the audio guy and the cast members every day, and that turns into a relationship.

A cameraman hides his face under a baseball cap and behind a camera. People don't know him. Same with the director or producer, who's always in the background as an "authority" figure.

But an audio person's face is exposed to the world. The cast members may look at him and smile, and he smiles back. The kids crack a joke -- the camera guy may miss it while getting a cutaway shot -- but the audio guy hears it and laughs, and the kids now consider him a friend.

Because of this, your audio person is the main STORY ally. He hears everything, and he is more apt to know what is going on with your overall story arcs than your cameraperson, director or producer.

In noisy scenes, the audio engineer is the only person who really knows what happened. Both the director and cameraman have tiny earplugs with which to listen, but the audio guy wears big cans on his head.

During an interview, the cameraperson must think about image, exposure, when to zoom in and out...as well as content. The cameraperson is sometimes too burdened with the immediate challenges to see the overall.

But once the audio person is happy with his sound set-up, his only job is to LISTEN INTENTLY. He may even enjoy the interview process and see where every question will go in the show.

He may have his own questions -- and better approaches to get the answers than the director.

Because of this, good audio people help drive stories forward. The audio person may know the cast better than anyone!

The Dance

The camera is the more glorious job. Plus, the audio engineer often looks like just he's following the camera around.

However, the two jobs are equal in importance.

Depending on the situation, one job may become more important than the other. For B-roll, the audio is less important. In a dark scene with few available shots but a great story on microphone, the audio is more important.

When the cast members sky-dive, for instance, all production on the ground stops and all eyes are on the audio engineer. He is waiting for the skydivers with microphones to come into range so he can hear what is going on. He is the first to know whose chute opened right away and who had problems. At this point, the audio engineer is the only one who knows the story.

The trouble is, audio is so easy to overlook. No one even knows that audio is there...until there's a problem and there's no audio, and suddenly there's no more story.

The audio person must also get the sound while simultaneously avoiding the darting and leaping shooter. They move in tandem, back and forth, at the same time.

It's important that they get along and treat one another with respect. It doesn't work if the shooter thinks the audio engineer is just there to "add the audio" to his shots.

THE DIRECTOR

The job of the director on a reality show is much more nebulous than the other positions.

On a feature film shoot, nothing rolls until the director says action.

On a reality shoot, shooters are expected to shoot something interesting when it happens -- if they waited for a director to arrive, a lot of great material would be missed.

Also, when the shooter is experienced, everyone already has a very good idea about what needs to be shot and why.

So... what does a director do on a reality shoot? ***He or she determines what the overall stories are with the producer, story editors and the other directors, then "directs" the crew and pushes the cast to get those stories.***

While the crew is gathering the stories, the directors and story editors and producers are endlessly discussing it.

Which interesting character is emerging? Who is fading away and needs to be pulled out? What story arcs are developing? What can be done to help the stories unfold?

In addition, what events are coming up that we should plan for? Can we streamline shooting? Should we change the approach on an upcoming shoot?

This means the directors and producers are often in story meetings -- either in the field, or on the phone.

Sometimes they are discussing immediate concerns, and sometimes they are discussing long-term decisions about story arcs for the whole series, not just what is happening that day.

Preparing the Crews and Directing their Attention

The director alerts the crews to what stories are happening and what plans have been made to make sure that stories happen.

The director must then inspire the crews to adopt the same creative ideas discussed in the story meetings.

If the directors did not do that, the crews would just shoot "what happens." The director may want to focus on one cast member that day, despite everything else that's happening, to draw that person out.

Another cast member may be charismatic and loud and a show-stealer. It's easy to keep shooting that person -- until the director changes the crew's focus to shoot the other people in the group -- to get their reaction to the charismatic show stealer.

Ultimately, this is what directing is -- to direct everyone's attention to one particular cast member or moment.

Most important, the director must communicate why he's directing everyone to follow one story or person. That way it's clear and everyone participates.

Keep tabs on what they get, and what they didn't get.

Because it's a documentary show, there is no second take. The director keeps track of what material the shooters got, and what story material they missed.

The director and producer then must develop a plan to make the story work without the missing material, or develop a plan to get it the next time.

Work with the story editor(s) to get story arcs

Every cast member has a story...sometimes several stories. Those stories each have a beginning, a middle, and an end.

The director must work with the story editor in the field and/or back in the post production office to track all the stories as they are taking place.

He must look for the next beat in each cast member's story, and draw his crew towards that new development.

He also must do what he can to make the next story beat take place. He doesn't want stories to just fade away.

Write all this up in the Director's Notes

He keeps track of all the work he is doing in his daily director's notes, which are the main tool the story department and the executive producers use to track the show's daily progress.

Each day, a novice editor may cut a "daily reel." He may use the director's notes as a guide. The producer and executive producers and story editors watch that daily reel and read those director notes each day.

If the director chooses to eliminate something from his director's notes, then it won't make the "dailies" reel. The story editor won't care as much about it, and it probably won't make the show.

This is where the director is the first "stop-gap" who prevents the LA office from being flooded.

A crew can work like crazy shooting material, but if the director doesn't think it's worth putting in his notes, then there's a good chance the material will be ignored.

This is why the director and the crew must always be on the same page. The shooter may think he is "saving the day" by shooting extra material. He may even ignore the director. But if the director doesn't include them in his notes, all his hard work was for nothing.

It's easier on everyone if the director and crew constantly talk about what they are shooting and why. (There is more on director's notes in a separate section.) ***Interviews***

The director and/or producer interviews each of the cast members.

Interviews are crucial to the process for several reasons. There is more on interviewing in the separate interview section.

DURING SHOOTING HE/SHE MUST ALSO:
Watch as scenes unfold.

The director is watching and taking notes, determining whether there is a worthwhile "scene" -- enough to add to a story.

Keep the shooter posted about changes to the scene.

Maybe an angry cast member is about to enter the room. The shooter needs to know this so they can drop back to a wide shot and include that new cast member as they enter the scene.

Help the camera people streamline their shots.

The camera shooter is mentally "editing" the scene as he shoots. So is the director. The director may need to remind the shooter to get certain crucial shots -- an establishing shot or a reaction shot, for instance.

Sometimes the director knows the scene will end before the shooter does. Sometimes they must leave the scene and go somewhere else, fast...which only the director knows about.

NOTE: New shooters may require a lot of directing. More experienced shooters need very little, and may prefer to be left alone.

But because the director ultimately has more story-telling responsibility, the shooter must defer to the director.

But once the scene has ended, the director must be able to defend his choices to the shooter. The shooter might insist he got the wide shot, but the director may insist otherwise.

Refer to the footage. At the end of the day they can check the footage out on the monitor and talk through the two different versions of how you'd each edit the scene.

These discussions can happen early in the production, and by the third week, everyone will be on the same page.

These discussions generally occur when the scenes are lukewarm or vague, when something is not quite working.

But when something great is happening, there's never a doubt about what's worth shooting. Then the director sits back and keeps quiet and lets the shooter get the shots.

ANOTHER NOTE:

Sometimes on reality TV shows an experienced shooter is teamed with an inexperienced director, or vice-versa. This levels out the experience across two crews, so there isn't one crew that is super-experienced and another that is new and struggling.

For this reason, it's especially important for the directors and the shooters to talk.

YET ANOTHER NOTE:

When you're on a well-run movie-set, a director often sits around waiting while everyone else works hard. But that's the way it should be, because if the director is good, he has done most of his work beforehand.

The same goes for a symphony conductor. In concert, he's just waving his baton. Plus, the musicians have probably played that piece of music thousands of times -- what do they need him for anyway?

The truth is, the conductor has done most of his work already, choosing the music, arranging, editing, coaching, cajoling, rehearsing, re-arranging, rehearsing again...

Then when it comes time for the actual concert he's mostly a cheerleader, reminding the musicians about a single creative vision about the music that they all now share.

When you're on a movie set, if the director is running around pointing, it usually means he's screwed up or is unprepared. He's also burning money, because production is so expensive.

The same goes for a director on a reality show. If he's done all his work before-hand, he can be relaxed during production and just focus.

A good director is also so tuned into the crew that he can communicate with mere glances. They have a secret code of clicks and single words to change camera angles and to start and stop scenes.

If the director must ask for something more than twice, something is wrong. When the crew in general complains that too much "chatter" is going on over walkie-talkies, it means that people aren't communicating.

Also, there is a good chance that the crew is working too hard shooting material that won't be used.

STORY PRODUCERS

The senior story producer (often the Co-EP) and the story producers watch all the footage and write the outlines and scripts for each episode, and create the overall "bible" that tracks the cast members' stories over the entire season.

They are constantly searching the director's notes, the dailies, and the raw footage for stories that have beginnings, middles, and ends.

They then plot out those stories so they can blend together into an interesting episode...and then blend with all the other episodes into an overall series that has its own story arc with a beginning, middle and end.

For this reason, the story department is thinking about the story all the time.

Most reality TV episodes have an A-story and a B-story that somehow fit together -- perhaps one is serious, perhaps one is funny.

Therefore, the story department only wants a scene if they know it can fit into an overall story arc somehow. Does it go anywhere? Does it advance a plot? Reveal something new about a cast member?

Many times, reality TV crews shoot scenes that don't end up fitting into an overall story.

Just because a scene is funny, for instance, doesn't mean it's worth putting in a show. This scene must somehow progress to other scenes over the course of days or weeks.

If there is a great scene, the story editors put it on a scene card and pin it to a bulletin board. If no other scene cards end up alongside it, that "scene" becomes and orphan and just sits there. The best orphans end up as credit beds.

Likewise, if a cast member delivers the same scene over and over again, that doesn't mean those scenes will make it into an episode either.

For instance, if a cast member gets into the same argument every day with her boyfriend, it gets boring quickly. Their relationship must change into something different, or perhaps the other cast members have to get involved. Otherwise, there's no story.

The story producers want the crews to think the same way they do. The crews should think about getting great scenes, and then anticipating what the next scene might be.

They should also be aware of when a scene isn't going anywhere. That way they can stop shooting and try a new approach or look for another scene elsewhere.

The Senior Story Producer (often the Co-EP) is the Senior Field Producer's (often the show runner/EP) mirror image back in the home office.

The Producer in the field works hard to make sure great stories get shot, without breaking the budget.

The Post Producer in the home office works hard to get those stories into edit bays and turned into episodes that can be broadcast...without breaking the budget.

The Producer in the field manages the shooters, the directors, the PAs, the audio engineers, the location managers. When there's a problem because a story or a cast member isn't working out, the Producer deals with it.

The Post Producer in the home office manages the story producers, the editors, the assistant editors, the music supervisor, the clearance and legal department. When there's a problem because a story or a cast member isn't working out in the edit bay, the Post Producer deals with it.

The overall Producer must deal with it as well, but because he is in the field with his own problems, the Post Producer takes over on his behalf and they communicate by phone.

So when the EP is in the field, everyone who works in post looks to the Co-EP as the person in charge. When the Producer returns from the field, the two Producers share responsibility and authority...although the overall Producer is first among equals.

EDITORS

Editors get an outline written by the story department and an edit system full of footage. Their job is to use the outline as a blueprint and build the story.

In that sense, editors feel like construction workers, slowly and methodically building the house.

Sometimes the house goes up very quickly and easily. Sometimes the story is harder to tell and it takes a long time to build a decent episode. Oftentimes, it's not obvious from the outline or the material what will be easy to edit and what won't.

If there is a big problem, the editor can't ask for another story. The story department has plans for all the stories -- there are none left over.

The editor can sometimes find another story within the existing material, or a different angle on the same story. But that new story or angle must fit into the overall series that the story department is building. He/She can't go off on his own.

Ultimately, each editor must make the story in his or her edit bay work...somehow. He/she may need to prop it up with music, or search for B-roll shots, or add an extra scene or interview bites. The episode must work.

For this reason, editors often feel like authors as well. They get very attached to every shot and every line in their show, and they know how each edit helps build the story they are trying to tell.

Telling a good story takes time. In fictional-based TV that time is spent BEFORE production, in story meetings and in the weeks it takes to write a script.

In reality-based TV, that time is spent AFTER production, in the story department and in the edit bays. A good story takes over ten weeks to do -- either writing it as fiction, or outlining and editing it in a reality show.

SECTION TWO:
TRICKS OF THE TRADE

This next section reveals some "tricks of the trade" used on reality TV shows. Some are particular to certain jobs -- but they all help streamline production and help the crew tell better stories.

A lot of these "tricks" also give the crews more story-telling responsibility, and it makes everyone's job more rewarding.

VIDEO MAP

Before the start of shooting, the production team does a video tour of the entire "location" for the post production department.

We draw a detailed map for the post-production department to go with the video tour.

We identify north, south, east and west...and point out where the sun rises and where it sets.

After the post-production team watches the helpful video tour they will know where they are whenever they look at footage.

The production crew and the post production department will give each location a name -- and only one name, with only one spelling.

The "Mardi Gras room" at the Real World House can't also be known as the "Party room" or as "Melissa's room." If a location gets logged with more than one name then searches become impossible. Work gets lost.

As the show goes on the characters will establish more "locations" themselves...thus requiring you to update your video tour. If someone always goes outside to smoke under the street lamp, then that will also become a location with a name.

This also goes for "outside" locations -- if they always go to the same bar, or where they work. If they encounter the same people there, those people must be identified quickly.

If they are identified incorrectly in the field or logged incorrectly in post, that work may be lost.

INTERVIEW LOCATIONS AND LOOKS

A wonderful locale gives you tremendous production value. With one shot you can tell the audience where you are and stun them with a great shot.

At the same time, most interviews end up as v.o., and most of the shot is never seen.

This is the dilemma of the "interview location." On one hand, if the cast is in Africa or at Mt. Rushmore, you want the audience to know that.

On the other hand, the editor generally prefers a tight shoulder shot for interview bites, that's because the eyes tell the story, not the background.

Also, if they are talking about what happened at the bar the night before, the stunning mountain vista behind them has nothing to do with the story they are telling.

It's tough for a production crew to work their way to some exotic interview location, and then see most of the interview not used, or re-framed in post so the background isn't really seen.

Before the producers, directors and the DP decide where the interviews should be, they determine how many of that week's questions will specifically tie in with the background shots.

If they are doing questions that cover several weeks, there is a chance that very few "stunning shots" will end up in the final shows. The interview location should be neutral and easy for the crew to handle.

If they are only going to be in that stunning location for a brief period of time and they need high production value, then it may be worth it for the crew to climb that mountain.

WHAT IS B-ROLL ANYWAY?

What is B-roll, and why do they call it B-roll? It comes from news producing shot on early videotape. When a news team arrives at a fire, they want to get the story done as quickly as possible. So they concentrate on getting the story on two different tapes: the A-roll...and then the B-roll.

The A-roll has the "story." The reporter does his stand-up, all the interviews with the firemen, the frightened tenants and the angry neighbors. They also get any amazing shots of the burning building as it's tumbling to the ground right in front of them.

In a rush, the reporter might even write track narration and read it into the camera. All this goes on the A-roll tape. It holds the skeleton of the story.

Once that is done, the shooter pops out that tape, and pops in a new one, then rushes around and gets "B-roll " shots.

These are the beautiful shots of the fire, of the tortured faces, of burnt charred bodies being loaded into the paddy wagons, the turning red lights on top of police cars, a little girl crying, the water flooding down the street carrying away the sins of the city...

The point is, once the A-roll is done, the news producer CAN AT LEAST TELL A STORY. The news producer in the field must gauge the situation carefully; how much time should she give the cameraperson to get all these other creative shots? After all, they must get this story on the air within two hours.

Eventually, the producer yells at the cameraperson, "We've got enough shots! Let's move!"

They then rush back to the TV station and hurry into an edit room. The editor takes the A-roll, and quickly edits the skeleton story information out like a script -- the reporter's introduction, the voice-over narration, the tragic interviews, and the final stand-up.

They now have a news story...for the radio. If you closed your eyes and listened, it would be a complete story, but if you watched it, there are huge black holes and very few pictures of the fire.

The segment producer then calls for the show producer to come in and take a quick "listen." The boss looks in, hears the story and looks at the clock and makes his decision.

"There's ten minutes until the 5 p.m. news...give me a two-minute tease version for the 5 show, then cut a longer five-minute version for the 6 p.m. show. And give me a ten second promo to lead off the broadcast."

He then walks out. The editor then shortens the story to two minutes...and reaches for the "B-roll " tape. He edits in pictures as fast as he can, just to cover the black holes. He might like the shot of the streaming water, but there's no time -- he settles for the charred bodies and the exploding car, lays them over the black holes and hands out the tape. It barely makes broadcast.

People phone the station and complain how insensitive and cruel the 5 p.m. story was...plus it didn't make sense.

The station manager yells -- until he realizes they got killer ratings and the whole town is watching the carnage.

Meanwhile, the editor is still cranking in the edit bay, using every second to create the new five-minute version for the 6 p.m. broadcast. For the longer version, he uses the best B-roll pictures, he stretches out the pace, he shows the crying little girl, and uses slow-motion shots of the spinning red lights and the streaming water. He makes the story not just tragic, but poignant. The five-minute version airs at 6 p.m. and people cry.

Months later, the news producer submits the 6 p.m. broadcast of the fire story for Emmy consideration...and wins.

It's the same story. It's the same script. But one version sucks and the other wins an Emmy. What made the difference? The B-roll tape and the amount of time in the edit room.

But the B-roll is not as important as the A-roll tape, because the A-roll tape has the story.

HOW B-ROLL WORKS ON A REALITY SHOW

Ultimately, reality stories are shot by someone with a video camera on their shoulder, getting basic documentary "coverage" of wide shots, medium shots, close-ups and cutaways...like ALL documentary shows.

It's the "B-roll" shots that will give the show a separate look...a consistent look, and it is an opportunity for the directors and shooters to give the show a style.

Rise has a look, and so does **Homeland**. So do reality TV shows. We sometimes shoot B-roll on film, sometimes from helicopters, drones, we have done time lapse shots, we use digital cameras, underwater cameras, we add effects in the edit bay -- all to make sure the show looks unique.

At the same time, beginning shooters or trainees often shoot B-roll first. This means there is a wide variety and quality of B-roll material.

What invariably happens is that certain shoot days become editor favorites because they have "gold"...while other days get ignored.

On other shows, like moving competition shows, the production is constantly moving and changing. Shooters work ten hours straight grabbing all the shots they can before the show leaves town to another location.

This means B-roll gets buried. Editors end up using the shots that are easiest to find, instead of digging deep into the bins from previous shoot days for the gold the shooter may have gathered.

The production crew gets frustrated because good work isn't being used. The post crew is frustrated because it takes so long to find a decent shot.

Here's what the production crew should keep in mind to make sure good work gets used.

B-ROLL VS. STORY VS. INTERVIEW

In the rush of production there may be confusion about how to organize material and cards. If there is confusion in the field, it gets carried over into post and work gets lost. So let's clarify:

Label all cards as one thing and one thing only.

A story card has story material on it. Anytime you are following any cast member around, that card is a story card and only a story card.

If you are shooting beautiful exterior shots of the house to use as "B-roll establishing shots," then that card is a B-roll card and only a B-roll card...even if a cast member walks through the frame.

But let's say a cast member runs out chasing another cast member and a fight breaks out. Then the B-roll shooter is obligated to stop taking pretty pictures and to follow the action.

That B-roll card is now NO LONGER A B-ROLL CARD. It has become a STORY card, because the shooter is shooting STORY MATERIAL.

The B-roll on that card should be considered lost. It is as if that B-roll never existed. The same goes for adding B-roll shots to any story card, for any reason.

"Why?" people ask. "We're working hard in the field, and there are loggers back in LA -- isn't it their JOB to find my great shots?"

The answer is NO. The story producers are not having as much fun as the people in the field are. They are slaving away in cubicles logging images of other people experiencing life in a mansion or having adventures in the great outdoors.

What should a story producer do when presented with a card that has an interview, and some B-roll, and some story, and then some more B-roll? I can guarantee he is not thinking about how great the shots are. He is cursing.

Months later, let's say an editor needs a great shot of the cast van driving by. She will not stop and think, "I'm bored with these shots. I bet there's some card somewhere out there in that great media river we are creating, a card with just the right shot I need! Let's take a half an hour to find it!"

She will go and grab shots from a bin that says, "B-roll of passing shots of the cast van." She will not think twice about it -- she doesn't have the time.

If you want your work to be used, it must be presented to the Story Department and the editors in a form that is so easy to understand that they have no choice but to use it.

An interview card is only an interview card. It can have two interviews, but nothing else. If there is anything else on the card, it will be ignored.

A story card is king. If you are shooting a B-roll card and then shoot a story, consider all that B-roll lost. If you want your great work to be used, do the B-roll again on another B-roll card.

Be Specific with your B-roll shots.

To really make sure your B-roll work gets used, be specific. Shoot an entire card of B-roll of only one type...big exterior shots of the house...small interior shots of photos and knick knacks...or all phone cutaways...all rainy day shots...all flowers...

There is a tendency to consider "B-roll" fun. Let's grab a camera and wander around and shoot some cool shots!

But if the bin says, "General B-roll," the editors reach for it last. Be super specific and your work will be used.

Be specific with your camera moves as well. Static, slow moves, and fast moves.

Also, if you are trying a complicated "move," don't just roll. Practice the move, then hit "record." Shoot the move at different speeds a few times, and then stop.

If there is too much stuff on the card, the editor gets frustrated. There are good shots, then bad ones, then good ones, and then long pauses...and then the editor gives up trying to figure out what the shooter was thinking and she just uses a still shot.

Many editors look at B-roll clips backwards. Why? Because editors assume that a cameraperson's best "move" is the last one. They assume that the shooter was trying something difficult and stopped when he or she was happy. Be careful about continuing to shoot the same shot after you've gotten something great -- it may not get used.

Be careful about passing the time by shooting B-roll. Sometimes there is downtime on production and everyone is waiting. The camera crew wants to feel useful, so they start shooting B-roll of...seagulls, let's say.

It keeps the crew sharp and working, and everyone stays "in practice." The shooter tries to capture a moment of seagulls swooping down, and then rising up...and then settling.

The shooter really concentrates and after ten minutes of shooting gets one cool amazing shot. He now lets the P.A. try. It's a learning experience, and the P.A. tries something new.

The entire experience for the crew has been a good one. They're communicating and working together and learning.

The card is labeled, with no explanation, and put in a box and sent back to L.A. -- where it causes pain and agony in the story department.

The logger watches and logs an entire card of seagulls rising and falling. He complains to his colleagues about his boredom. What were they thinking? He finally gives up and fast-forwards through the one great shot on the card.

BUT! All is forgiven if you write it down on the camera logs or slate your cards. If there is only one good shot on the card, write that on the card, include it on the camera report, or stand in front of the camera and say it into the lens.

Then the logger knows what's up with the card and will know how to use your work.

If there was a killer sunset shot that was going by so fast that you had to put it on an interview card, then include that on the log so people will know to use it!

"Slating" the cards at the front works the best. Stand in front of the camera and say, "we're doing all seagull shots now, and a P.A. is practicing..."

Then the logger and the editor knows what's up. Just saying it as audio doesn't work, because an editor will look at most B-roll cards in fast motion anyway.

But if you stand in front of the lens and announce what's up, the editor is sure to stop. First off, the crew is always interesting -- and second, the editors will know you have something to say.

If you follow these guidelines then you have a much greater chance of creating B-roll "gold."

Remember:
1)Label all the cards either story, interview or B-roll.
2)Don't combine different elements. Don't put B-roll on an interview or story card.
3)Be super specific with your B-roll so that it gets used. No "general" B-roll.

4)Don't let the camera just roll. Practice your moves --
then roll. If you nail it, stop there, or tell us.

5)Don't just pass the time by shooting B-roll for the
fun of it -- unless you admit that's what you're doing.

6)"Slate" your shots with an on-camera explanation.
Make sure your camera logs show what is on the card,
so that loggers will know what to look for. This will
insure that any buried treasure can be found.

Here is some story specific B-roll to keep in mind:

Transitional B-roll

It's always difficult in a reality show to transition
from one scene to another. The editor must find an
elegant way to show a passage of time and space in
just a few seconds. He may also need to set up the
mood of the new scene as well.

Aerials always work -- they open the show up,
they let the audience catch their breath, and then you
move onto the next scene.

Another way to do this is to string a montage of
pictures together, set to music.

But what also works great is B-roll that
specifically shot to help act as a transition...a backlit
shot of distant figures walking into the sunset...that's a
potential end of an Act, for instance.

It could be an extreme low angle shot of people all
tumbling out of the cast van, their feet huge in the
foreground. Since you can't see clothes that well and
the location is nonspecific, this shot can help end the
"voyage" from one place to another.

A slow move may start or end of an Act. Fast moves end up in quick transitions from place to place, or when we remind people that we're back where we left off.

Think of how your B-roll shots work in the story, and work to make them help transition the story.

For instance, long slow moves on signs never get used. The longest establishing shot in any reality TV show was at most eight seconds. If you are designing a complicated move longer than five seconds it may not get used.

Keep this in mind, especially on the expensive days when you're using helicopters or jibs.

Extreme wide shots look great, but if it takes too much time for people to walk through frame, it gets cut, especially if you are doing a half-hour show.

P.O.V. (POINT OF VIEW) shots

P.O.V. shots can help establish a place very quickly. They can also cover a voice-over and help jump around from place to place.

Whenever a house or a new location is being show on a reality TV show, P.O.V. shots often act as "the tour."

You can also adopt a cast member's "mind-set" when you are shooting P.O.V. If they are scared or anxious, the P.O.V. moves would be different than if they are just happy and exploring some new location.

Remember that all transitions and B-roll and P.O.V. shots get cut down to very short time spans. If you want to do P.O.V. moves, make sure you do fast version to go with the slower ones.

B-roll particular to the stories you are telling

If a cast member is afraid of the water, it helps to shoot some B-roll that makes the water look threatening.

That can be tough, if the water is a pristine beautiful lake surrounded by mountain wild flowers, but if the shooter finds a way to make the lake look scary, then we can use that B-roll to make that cast member's fear more apparent.

Later, when she conquers her fear of the water, we can use beautiful B-roll to show her fear is gone.

If you keep these story opportunities in mind when you shoot B-roll, then the editors do less work constructing the story in the edit bay.

NOTE: An experienced camera shooter on a reality show already thinks about these shots, and incorporates them into the A-Story footage.

For instance, let's say the cast is all going to a bar. The shooter may capture generic transition shots suggesting they are going someplace...people putting on coats at the door...feet getting into the car...we see faces and reaction shots...we establish the bar as they walk up. We see a cutaway shot of the sign, and we see a P.O.V. shot walking through the crowd and up to the bar.

Then we catch up with the cast members just as they sit down and start talking. We now see the scene unfold.

We have all the "B-roll" shots we need, and they've been seamlessly incorporated into the same footage that holds the story.

This is the mark of a good reality shooter who is always thinking about the story and the coverage while the story is taking place.

They know how their work ends up in the final show, and they get better material by shooting less.

The other B-roll material still need to be shot, but the editor will choose the most shots from the main shooting.

A reality TV show always looks the best when it feels like you're there as it happens.

ANOTHER NOTE: You may have an ingenious plan to stalk a cast member with special cameras and microphones, but it'll take time to perfect your strategy.

If you don't share your vision, both on the camera notes and with a "speech slate," an inexperienced producer might fast-forward through this new footage with the imperfect new approach and label it UNUSEABLE.

You may get a killer scene, but not enough cutaways and reaction shows. You have a plan to grab those shots from the cast the next time they are in that room...but you must TELL everyone what you are doing...otherwise that second card makes no sense to anyone and the producer will label it UNUSEABLE.

Sometimes you will get great audio but a lousy image, but you keep rolling. Maybe you're pretending not to shoot, or maybe the camera is covered with a raincoat.

The story producer wants to get through his quota of ten hours of material for the day. If one hour has nothing but lousy shots because he thinks the shooter messed up, he will be thrilled to fast-forward through your crucial audio and label the footage UNUSEABLE. Use your camera logs. Slate your cards!

THE FIRST TWO WEEKS OF SHOOTING

During the first week of shooting, everyone will be running around like crazy, shooting everything.

You won't know if you're getting good material or not -- and then suddenly the story will change. It's the start of the flood. But here are several ideas that will keep you focused:

The first week of the show is about getting used to the new surroundings.

This is what all the cast members will be going through, and what your 1st and 2nd episodes will be about anyway.

Follow all the business of "getting to know each other." That includes greetings, first impressions, first meals, first greetings, and fears. When you see those events happen, follow them.

Don't worry too much about important people explaining things. On a reality show, there's often an expert who gives a tour or a teacher who leads a lesson.

This often happen at the beginning of a season or episode when cast members must "learn the ropes," or learn the rules.

But each show is only 22 minutes long -- there's no time for a lesson. So focus not on the lesson as much on everyone's reactions to the lesson. If there is good audio and a few shots of the teacher, the lesson will be cut down in editing to thirty seconds.

But if one cast member loves the lesson and another one hates it, then it can become a bigger part of the story.

Where am I and how did I get here?

The first episode must quickly set up the cast members, their previous lives, and the new place where they will all be interacting.

The rest of the episode is them getting used to each other and their new surroundings.

First episodes are tough because they can quickly become a laundry-list. Meet cast member 1, now meet cast-member 2...now here's a montage of the house where they will all stay...

All of this is important, but it's not STORY...it's backstory. The story doesn't really start until all this information is out of the way.

To make up for this, the producer and the directors work hard to create situations so that backstory emerges at the same time story takes place.

For example, sometimes in reality TV shows new cast members meet on a train and talk together. One may have a key to "the house." The scene isn't about trains and it's not about keys...it's still about getting used to one another, but it's now more visually interesting and the back story gets hidden into some larger scene with a cool train in it.

It's your first time only once.

The first week is about FIRSTS. The first handshake, the first hint of sexual attraction, the first joke, the first meal together.

All those FIRSTS will only happen once, so focus on them. Those other moments will come back...but it's your first time only once. They may also reveal some secret fear or desire that's worth tracking.

Don't be afraid of tidbits.

During the first few days of shooting, you may feel frustrated because you're not getting whole scenes -- you're getting little tidbits. A moment here, a tiny meeting there.

Don't be discouraged. Those little thirty-second tidbits might be best for a first episode anyway. The first episode is often about tidbits -- after all, you have to introduce all the cast members in thirty minutes.

If you get a real meaty scene the first or second day, be proud...but there is a good chance that the story department will save it for episode 202.

PROBLEMS YOU'LL ENCOUNTER

During the first two weeks of shooting, everything is crazy. The crews are getting used to one another, so is the cast, and a dozen stories are developing, all at once. Some will lead to story arcs with an Act 2 and Act 3, while others will die.

Meanwhile, the footage is coming into the post department and the frustration in the field is often there for everyone to see. Here are some common problems from the first two weeks.

1) Always arriving late

Because the crew isn't the Mission Impossible stealth squad yet, it takes that much longer to clue in on a story, and it takes that much longer for technical adjustments.

They arrive on a scene just as it's ending. Plus the cast members aren't comfortable yet, so they clam up when the stampede arrives. Don't rush it. You'll get there. Or get there first and just wait.

2) Rushing through the shots

The shooter may be getting direction from two directors and the DP, and they all may be contradicting one another, or the shooter may be behind understanding what's going on the scene.

What ends up on the footage is rushed shots. The camera zooms in focuses, then zooms out, holds for less than a second, the shifts to someone else. The shots don't hold...and when they do that's just the moment when the cast member gets up out of the chair and leaves frame.

The shooter often doesn't realize he's doing it -- he's so amped up, a second feels like an eternity, so he's changing shots fast, sometimes too fast and yet he's missing everything. Just slow down and listen.

3) Following everything too closely

The shooter arrives on the scene and is ready to work! He gets right in the mix and is shooting away, struggling to get those shots. The cast members walk upstairs...then into a room...and then downstairs...and the shooter is right there the whole time, working, just inches away.

But there's no distance, no sense of the place, no long shots, no parting shots where people leave frame. It's hard to edit these scenes because there are no establishing shots. There's no distance. It's all one emotion -- tight and close.

4) Not enough reaction shots

The shooter tends to shoot only the person talking, and not the people listening. This makes it hard to shorten the scene, or give the scene any point of view.

The scene could be poignant, dramatic, or comedic -- but the reaction shots tell the audience how to feel.

To the shooter's credit, the cast members are also camera shy at first. The first two weeks are overwhelming for them. When a camera is right next to them they tend to shift, and turn away. There are a lot of profile shots, or quarter profiles, or even the backs of people's heads.

5) *Not being comfortable with the environment*

Before each Real World season the crews go into the rooms and shoot footage with each other, just trying to figure out where the good shooting spots are in the room.

The same thing happens on road shows and competition shows. Everyone tries to anticipate where the shooters and audio people should stand and where the directors should hide.

Then production starts and all that work gets blown to bits. The cast members all decide to hang out in the tiniest room, with the worst light, and the sound of traffic outside.

Phone calls should be easier, right? Wrong. There's always one guy who lies on the floor, face down, his head in shadow while his feet are well-lit.

It turns out that all the "great" spots for shooting weren't so great after all. Suddenly the crew must adapt.

There is no solution -- there will always be problems in the first two weeks of shooting. The struggle for post-production is that the first and second episodes that set up the whole series often must be invented from the footage in these first two weeks.

The one overall solution is to remember the basics while in the midst of the shooting. Relax. Don't rush up to the scene, don't rush through your shots, get the long shot and the reaction shots and let people leave the frame. Don't stay super close and use the long end of the lens. Stay sensitive to the cast and let them get used to you.

You can also spot check footage and see if you got what you hoped to get.

After Two Weeks

After two weeks, the crew is usually working together well. They get to scenes ahead of time, they're ready technically, and they cover the scene well.

The cast members understand the rhythms of the process and they let the crew do their work.

If the crew talks about these things at the end of the shooting day, they'll get better that much faster and shoot less in the process.

OTHER SHOOTING NOTES

New shooters are visually oriented. New camera shooters will be drawn to the most visually interesting image available, whether it's a horse or a pretty girl or someone yelling, even if it has nothing to do with the scene that needs to be covered.

Beginning shooters must learn to listen to what's going on and put themselves in the moment and not chase something simply because it's louder or brighter or more interesting visually.

What doesn't work:"
Cutaways" of hands

In some manual somewhere, someone wrote that when you are shooting a scene, it's good to shoot cutaways of hands. Editors hate them and always avoid them. It's always better to cut-away to a shot of someone listening, or looking, or even the long shot.

Sometimes a cut-away to the hands works, if the person is doing the dishes, or talking on the phone and playing with the phone cord. Other than that, shooting someone's hands doesn't work -- especially if they're engaged in a conversation.

The perfect progress of some on-going action

Cooking a meal...packing or unpacking a bag...eating a bag of candy...eating an ice-cream cone.

Oftentimes shooters feel obligated to get each step of an ongoing process.

Let's say a cast member is cooking. If a scene ends up getting through the story department and into an edit bay, it's strictly because of the conversation going on *around* that cooking.

Or maybe the scene is about the reason the cooking is taking place – maybe it's their last meal together, which again makes it about the cast members and not about the cooking.

The cooking itself will be summed up by the editor in just three or four shots...boiling water...a cracking egg...something coming out of the oven.

This is true even if the entire episode is about Thanksgiving dinner. Therefore you don't need to nail every shot of every step of the process -- pick shots that you can anticipate -- like something coming out of the oven -- and place yourself so that you're right there. The cast member knows what's up and will let you get that shot.

This is true of anything that involves a process. The editor will eliminate almost everything and cut the process down to its bare essence -- and concentrate instead on the faces and the emotion in the room.

If something dramatic is taking place, no one will notice that Joan had an ice-cream cone in one shot, and then three shots later it's gone and she's licking her lips. If there are enough shots of faces the editor can always make it work.

The only exception to this is if someone is performing some task badly. Their mess-ups, their spills, and their frustration turn the task into a comedy, and therefore worth shooting...and even in that case, their face and their body language will communicate that more than spilled food.

__Be careful about lessons, explanations and tours.__

The cast members will often encounter teachers or "mayors." The mayor is the reality TV code word for the authority figure in charge who must give the cast information.

A good mayor is funny, interesting, gives short concise statements, and then backs away. Anything more than that gets cut out.

For instance, in one Real World season, the cast members "boss" at the public access TV station worked gave them an hour long tour of the facility, then spoke to them for another hour. Reality TV used almost none of it in the final episode. Why?

Because the episode wasn't a video brochure for the public access station. It was about the cast member's reaction to their new job. In the show, they learned what their job was, and they reacted. End of story.

The same goes for long lessons and explanations, or anything that involves too much exposition.

Don't worry about "when" a scene is supposed to take place.

A reality show doesn't represent the true passage of time. Bob and Joan may have an on-going friendship/romance that stretches over many weeks.

Only after six weeks, let's say, is there enough of a story arc between these two characters to edit into a story.

During this same six weeks, let's say, Bob always bickers with Sam. That may make it into an episode three weeks prior to the Bob/Joan romance.

Since there is no way for the shooter to know when a scene is going to fall in the overall series, the shooter shouldn't feel obligated to tie scenes together in the field.

Sometimes a scene will end up in the edit bay -- a flirty love-scene between Bob and Joan. The scene is going well. Sam suddenly enters the room and stands off to one side. He doesn't add anything, he doesn't participate. He finally turns away.

But the shooter stays on Sam, and doesn't return to Bob and Joan. The editor is confused...

Until he looks back at the logs and previous material and learns that Bob and Sam had one of their long fight sessions an hour earlier, and now Sam has walked back into the house.

The shooter is still in the fight scene between Sam and Bob from two hours earlier. It's a good instinct to go for Sam. That fight was probably the most dramatic event of the day.

But if the fight doesn't continue, the shooter must go back to the scene he left, immediately. Sam and Bob will have their ACT 2 moment later.

There's no obligation stay with Sam, or try to incorporate Sam into the new scene by inventing some shot that gets all of them in together...the two scenes may be in completely different shows.

Stay with the scene, but work with the director.

The shooter's job is to capture the moment.

The director's job is to keep track of all the moments with all the cast members, and try to make sure the next moment happens.

The director is in an on-going daily dialogue with the producer, the story department and the executive producers.

If the moments aren't adding up to a show, or if some cast members aren't coming through, then the director must come up with a plan -- any plan -- to try and make the next thing happen.

If the shooter and director are in synch, then they can plan together what they should do.

That might be to keep shooting Sam after all, no matter where he is or what he's doing. That might be to stop shooting Sam altogether and to avoid him for several days. It might be to shoot half a scene and then walk away.

If the director and shooter aren't in synch, the director's attempts to gather more moments, or better moments, can piss a shooter off.

"I'm getting gold here, and the director is telling me to stop! Screw that, I'll shoot what I want. I know this story better than she does. They'll thank me for it later."

But if the shooter had to log that footage, view that material, then edit it together, he might feel different.

Oftentimes, editors come across moments when the shooter and the director are obviously at odds.

You can hear the shooter swear, or audibly sigh. You can see that the director wants the shooter to do something, but it's not clear what.

Sometimes the director's choice may even be a bad one, and the shooter is letting the director know. Sometimes the shooter does what the director wants, but only half-heartedly, and then returns to shooting the scene the way he first intended.

This is part of production and everyone must roll with it. But at the same time, that process doesn't happen only once. It happens again with the producers who must log it...with the story department who must watch it...and then again with the editor who must cut around it.

It's only a moment in the field, but Post Production will devote as much time and energy into this bad moment as to a moment that is "gold." Plus, everyone in post will experience it three times, not once.

Leap-frogging

Let's say the cast members are going somewhere -- on a fishing trip, for instance.

They get dressed. They get in the car. They talk about the trip in the car. They see the boat. They get on the boat. They drive in the boat to the fishing spot. They go fishing. Some people get sick. Other people catch fish. They drive the boat back. They get off the boat. They wait for the car. They get in the car. They talk about the fishing trip in the car on the way back. They get home.

Later that week, the crew also interviews them about the trip. Cutting away to an interview allows the editor to remove any step in the process.

So how much of all this will actually end up in the episode? Do you really need to shoot it all? The editor will hack out 90 percent of this. So why shoot all of it?

If you're invested in the story, it's easy to anticipate what's important and what's not.

Trips are usually about struggling to get there, being there, or struggling to get back. If the producer and director decide that the important stuff was already on the way out, there's no need to hump it like a foot solider to get everything on the way back. The editor will just cut to a sunset shot and the trip will be over.

This doesn't mean to put the camera down and have a beer. It just means that you don't have to carry the camera constantly, three feet away from the cast.

You can hang back at bit and listen -- see what's up with the cast members. Then if something big happens, you can get back in there.

Eliminate "process' steps like this as much as possible. It's easier on the cast members and it's easier on the crew, and it helps the story!

MORE STORY WITH LESS FOOTAGE

Mix it up. A devoted shooter may stick close to the cast members whenever they go out...always walking with them to the bar...sticking close at the bar...sticking close on the way home. Getting it all!

Soon the cast members anticipate what the crew will do. If something is bothering them, it's easy to avoid bringing it up in front of the cameras because the crew's behavior is so predictable. They just wait for a card change, or for that camera shooter to leave.

Mix up your shooting style. Shoot from far away. Pretend you're not shooting. Just roll on audio. Shoot them on the way there, but give the cast member a break on the way back...and see if their habits change. It may make something happen.

The shooter won't have to work so hard. You shoot less. The audio person will monitor the story progress, and then as a group, the crew can decide if the story requires the shooter to go back in full force. Everyone is more involved in the story, and there's more good material than mediocre.

Rely on audio more. Let's say it's a crowded bar scene, and all the cast members are there. You've gotten some good shots, but nothing new seems to be happening.

It's always very noisy and there are too many conversations going on and the cast members are too far apart.

Stop shooting and let the audio person monitor what's going on from some central location.

The cast members are more apt to relax and talk with whatever civilian bought them a drink. Romance may develop.

The audio person can monitor three conversations at once. If one is going absolutely nowhere, she can suggest swapping the radio mic to someone else.

Then, if something starts to happen, you can roll on just the audio. You can then back up this audio with long shots, silhouette shots, or shots of people facing away from the camera.

Just like the field biologist, you can now approach the gazelle slowly and move in for more shots. Hopefully, the gazelle will continue to graze and not bolt for the trees.

If something racy is going on, the long shots will add to the feeling of "voyeurism," which the audience enjoys. Because you've given a break to the cast members, the story has advanced a little -- perhaps towards romance. And you get back in and get the rest of the conversation.

You've shot less, you've gotten more story, and everyone was involved in the process.

The Floating Camera:

Sometimes a shooter enters "the zone." This is amazing to watch, so enjoy it. Let's say it's one of our female shooters. This is what will happen:

She is accepted by the cast members and is completely ignored. She hears and understands everything, and becomes part of the scene.

Her hand-held shot floats like a Steadicam, from wide shot into a carrying shot, into a two shot, then into a close-up, until someone walks by...stimulating another camera move into another person's face....

And she keeps going, is never goes out of focus, and it's constantly changing the frame.

It would take Martin Scorsese three days to design and shoot the same scene with a Steadicam, and the shooter got it all instinctively as it happens.

But it can't be planned -- it happens. Some shooters just have this gift. And when it happens, stay out of the way.

But what the crew needs to remember is that a three-minute "Steadicam" shot won't get used.

The shooter must end her shots. Let cast members leave the frame. Rest on a close-up. These are necessary, because they give the editor edit points.

It's hard for the shooter to hear this -- it's like telling Michael Jordan to stop shooting the basketball so much.

But her work has a better chance of being used if she can stop the floating camera, give the editor a cut point, and then continue on "in the zone" with a new shot. Three minute shots will get hacked up anyway, but a twenty second shot might make it into the show in its entirety.

The Static Camera:

Sometimes, a shooter refuses to move. They may have a cast member in a close-upshot and confessing some secret. The story is five minutes long and fantastic. And the shooter gets all of it! This is the opposite of the Floating Camera. It's the rock solid shooter who never budges.

And they've also given the editor no shots with which to work. How will the editor shorten this five-minute story? They'll need to use an interview, which lessens the impact of the scene anyway. That story is now diluted.

This happens mostly with beginning shooters. They shouldn't be reprimanded. It's a great instinct, because they're listening as well as shooting.

But they should be reminded that AUDIO GETS THE STORY. The audio engineer knows the story is important. He spotted the story first, because it was the audio from his microphone that got the shooter's attention and enticed the crew over in the first place.

Once the shooter finds that killer shot, he must get coverage. You may miss the shot of the wet tear rolling down the cheek, but the reaction shot from their best friend may be even better. Don't freeze.

"The Line":

Production classes and text books devote chapters to "the line." In a documentary there is no way to control the people in the scene, so you can't establish "a line." It's always changing, and the shooter is always adapting. So relax, there's no reason to worry about it.

It only changes when there's two-camera coverage on a scene. If you're at a lesson, one camera might shoot the teacher talking from the left side of the frame, while the other camera shoots the students yelling back from the right-hand side of the frame.

If you don't, when you cut the two scenes together, it will look like the teacher is talking to a group of people who aren't even facing him -- because they're actually facing the same direction he is.

Is this something you should worry about? Is this a crucial rule of filmmaking? Will the editing police come and put you in prison if your shots don't line up? NO! In fact, the editors DON'T CARE.

This isn't live TV. The scene will be edited.

Too often in production people mentally abandon the scene to worry about what's going to happen in the edit bay six months from now. The two shots won't even necessarily go together.

The editor may cut to the clock, cut to the long shot, cut to someone else talking in the other direction, and then cut to a listening shot from another lesson on another day...and in the show, it will look fine. The editor can even flop the shot in the AVID and change direction anyway.

This doesn't mean the camera should forget about frame direction at all. But if they have a great shot in one direction and no shot the other way, they shouldn't try to move, and they shouldn't stop shooting. By the time they get to their new spot, the scene may change yet again...so remind everyone to go with the flow.

Double Camera Coverage:

Let's say two cameras arrive on the scene, and you need to decide how to do double camera coverage. What do you do?

You defer to whoever is the senior shooter. That person is already in the midst of the scene. He can instantly see where both cameras should stand, and they will decide where the junior shooter should stand.

Maybe that will be back-to-back, or side to side, or across a table from each other.

Include the Other Cast Members:

A scene most often comes down to an interaction between two people...let's say Bob and Joan.

Sometimes there are three, but even then, the conversation is usually being dominated by two.

But the show is about ALL the cast members. When you look at the finished episodes of reality TV series, they always contain interview bites of the other people talking about what happened between Bob and Joan.

A good experienced shooter gets the coverage, and somehow remembers to look for that other person in the room, the observer who's watching. The shooter gets a cutaway of them listening, or shaking their head, or smiling.

That cast member is suddenly part of the scene, and is allowed to comment in interview. They were there and they get to comment. The camera is also giving them permission to participate, where in real life they may want to steer clear of Joan and Bob's discussion. (There's more on this later)

Use Your Own Secret Code:

Develop a communication short hand. Clicks on the walkie-talkie, glances, and one-word reminders. When you are shooting, the fewer the words the better. You can always talk later, after the moment is over.

USING THE POWER OF
THE CAMERA

For the crew, the camera is just a camera. But most people outside of the entertainment industry see the camera as something much more powerful.

When a camera is around, things are different. It means something special is happening. A lot of people want to be on TV -- it means that their lives matter.

Even after weeks of shooting, when the cast members and counselors are completely used to having cameras around them, that power never goes away. Everything they do is somehow significant because their lives are being recorded.

You can use this power to make your show better. If you forget about this power, it can make your show worse.

Starting and Stopping the Camera:

Most of the time, the cast members want to please you. They want to give you what you want. If you shoot them doing something, you are approving of what they are doing and they will continue to do it.

Let's say two people are having an argument. If they allow you to shoot their conflict, you are telling them that their argument is good. They will keep arguing.

People also talk in cycles. They make the same point again and again. The other person counters with their viewpoint again and again. That's why couples go to marriage counselors -- so they can learn to stop having the same argument over and over again.

If you keep shooting an argument, you may be reinforcing the two people to continue the same cyclical pattern. They want to get their point across to anyone -- and as long as you keep shooting it, you're acknowledging that their viewpoints are worth putting on TV.

The shooter keeps rolling, hoping the conversation will change or end. It doesn't. It goes on and on. It becomes a feedback loop -- the camera is reinforcing the argument and it's feeding back to the camera.

So what can you do? STOP SHOOTING. The conversation won't change...until you stop shooting.

The moment you stop shooting, the two combatants will receive a different message -- YOUR ARGUMENT IS NO LONGER WORTH PUTTING ON TV.

Because they seek your approval, they will change their argument. They might suddenly see the other's viewpoint, or raise the stakes. Something DIFFERENT will happen. I don't know whether this happens consciously or subconsciously, but it happens.

This is frustrating for dedicated shooters, because they'll shoot for hours, never moving, hoping to get every single moment of the argument.

The director hears the same argument three times, and pulls the shooter out of the scene -- and a moment later, the scene changes! The shooter is naturally frustrated. If he'd only been allowed to stay in there a minute longer, he'd have gotten the big change! The director blew it!

I insist the change happened precisely because the shooter stopped shooting. And there's still plenty of time to get this new "cycle" of the argument.

You send the camera back in, and the unspoken message is once again sent -- NOW YOUR ARGUMENT IS WORTH PUTTING ON TV AGAIN. The combatants will continue on this new cycle, even repeating the few lines the shooter missed.

And even if you missed a few crucial lines, so what? The editor will restructure their whole discussion a dozen different ways anyway.

Oftentimes an editor will receive an "argument" scene from the field, and it will be on six cards. After viewing the first two, the editor starts asking herself -- when will this argument end?

So she jumps ahead to the last bit of footage and sees the "end" of the argument. Now she knows where's she's going and what to look for. Most of the time, she'll use the just first bit of footage and the last bit anyway, and very little of the argument in between.

By starting and stopping, a director can condense the same argument down to one card out in the field -- and make this strange experience easier for everyone.

It can also drive the story forward. Once you have the same argument three times in three different places, that story beat is DONE. The story department needs the next installment on this drama.

This same phenomenon works in dozens of situations, not just with arguments.

If you're shooting somebody bungee jumping, they may freeze. They can't jump. The camera locks in on them. The director tells the shooter, "this is fantastic! Whatever you do, DON'T MOVE!"

The shooter doesn't move. Neither does the bungee jumper. The terrified jumper doesn't know what to do. He wants to back down, but the camera is expecting him to jump. He wants to please, but is terrified.

Plus, the camera is telling him on some subconscious level, YOUR FROZEN FEAR IS WORTH PUTTING ON TV. So the poor bungee jumper does the one thing he can do -- he allows his humiliating fear to endlessly feed the camera.

After a half hour of shooting the same shot of frozen fear, the exhausted shooter finally swears under his breath and lowers the camera to clean his fogged up lens and viewfinder -- and the guy jumps! Right then!

The director hates the shooter for missing the shot, and the shooter hates the jumper for picking that one moment to leap. But the jumper chose that moment to go precisely because the feedback loop had been broken.

Maybe he heard the shooter swear and curse, and thought he was causing "a problem." Maybe he was just glad the pressure was off. Maybe the jumper thought, "Oh my god, I'm no longer interesting! I'd better jump!"

One way around this feedback loop is to get another camera on the bungee jumper from another angle, and have the two shooters start and stop. That can prompt a reaction, speed up the process, make the jumper go faster, or give him permission to step off the bungee platform.

And all of this happens without ever telling the bungee jumper anything. No words are ever exchanged. The same goes for the arguing combatants.

So be aware of the feedback loop and make it work for you, not against you. Realize the length people will go to please the camera. People would rather hurt themselves than look weak or silly on TV, and they will put themselves in danger or humiliate themselves, all on your behalf.

The Camera as Cast Member

You can use this same power of the camera to make scenes happen for you as well.

Imagine the camera as a cast member -- an eighth member of the house. He's not just in the background watching, he's in the mix, always participating.

Let's say there's a room full of six noisy people and one shy cast member. Let's say the camera goes in and ignores the noisy people and focuses strictly on the shy person.

After a while, the conversation will turn to the shy kid. The others will want to participate in what the shy person and the "eighth housemate" are doing. In this way, you can make the story come to you.

This is how you make second acts and third acts happen for your stories. You've planted seeds in all your interviews, and now the crew is in the room, right next to the cast member in question, silently saying IT'S TIME TO TALK ABOUT THIS.

Although the crew is not saying anything, the camera is silently saying "I don't care how noisy you all are. I have plenty of shots of people being noisy. I want to involve this person in the show. This person is important. Deal with this person..."

This works. Where's it's most obvious is when the camera is shooting photographs on a mantle or a desk. The room is full of people talking, but the camera insists on shooting photos!

Within a minute, someone in the cast always ends up asking -- "who are those people in your photos, Bob?"

If the crew has already decided to do this already, it's a great technique to draw out Bob's backstory. Soon everyone is asking him about his pictures and where he's from, and it's all in scene.

This also works to draw out the quiet person, or to involve them in the show. It also gives an observer permission to participate in a scene.

Let's say Joan and Bob have the same argument every morning...and the camera shoots it every morning. Joan and Bob will continue to have the same argument and the shooter is wasting time, spinning his wheels.

Let's say in the third argument the shooter focuses instead on the other cast member trying to read the paper. He will be drawn into the story, or the others will be drawn towards him.

The focus of Joan and Bob's problem has shifted -- which many force Bob and Joan to shift as well.

It's easy to shoot a charismatic cast person. They're the loudest and brightest person in the room. But that only works for a little while. In the actual episode, the story will quickly turn to how the other cast members feel about the charismatic person. Do they like him? Hate him?

By shifting the focus to the quieter people, they give the important reaction shots that tell the audience how the charismatic people are being viewed.

If you stay with the loud person all the time, they won't change. But if you shift to the quieter people, the audience will see a new point of view, and the charismatic cast member may end of changing and adapting, trying to garner attention again.

This may seem like a subtle dynamic, but it's very powerful -- especially when romance is involved. People may not recognize how the camera can steer a story...until they're innocently holding hands with someone and the camera rushes over.

Then they know, the crew knows, the whole house knows -- LOOK! THESE TWO PEOPLE HAVE A RELATIONSHIP. Everyone is very aware of the camera's power then -- it's pushing a story -- maybe too powerfully.

Dealing with the Scene Stealer:

You can also use the power of the camera to reinforce or alter specific behavior. If there is one cast member who is a "drama king" or a "drama queen," you might get great material from them at first.

But after a few days you may notice that your drama queen has the talent to steal the attention away from whatever else is happening in the room. This isn't bad...until it's the only story that ever happens when the camera is around.

These people love the camera. They are experts at interrupting people at crucial moments, yelling from across the room, stepping in front of the lens, and basking gloriously in the limelight once the attention is on them.

If they're stealing scenes or behaving rudely, take the camera away. No comment is needed. Shoot everyone else in the room...and when they show up to steal focus, turn and leave.

Better yet, purposely put a microphone on them...then if they misbehave, immediately take it off them. Again, no comment is needed.

This isn't manipulative. If you were witnessing a normal conversation between two people (without a camera) and someone walked up, stepped in front of you and interrupted, your natural reaction would be to say, "Excuse me, I can't hear what these two people are saying. Would you lower your voice please?"

If they don't listen to you or respect you, your only option is to walk away. Do the same with the camera.

Other people will soon catch on, and leave as well. That person will change their behavior very quickly.

If you don't, then you are sending the message: YOUR RUDENESS IS WORTH PUTTING ON TV, and you will actually reinforce the behavior. And if other cast members believe that rudeness is what you want, then they will either tolerate it or start doing it themselves.

"Training" The Cast

During the first week, the cast members won't be used to the cameras, and the shooters won't be used to them.

But there will be one or two cast members whom the cameras love. They are not "scene stealers," by any means; but for whatever reason, they've got "it."

And what is "it?" Part of "it" involves knowing how to work with the camera. In the same way that there's a dance going on with the camera shooter and the audio engineer, there's also a dance going on between the cast members and the cameras.

The savvy cast member watches the crew and sees how they work, and changes his or her behavior in subtle ways to make it easier for the crew to follow them.

It's most apparent when it comes to the "reaction shot." Two cast members are having a conversation. Instead of stepping on another person's comment, the savvy cast member waits until the camera is pointed at them.

No one told them to do this -- they just seem to know what the camera needs.

You see it often in an edit bay. Someone will repeat himself or herself, because they want to make sure their line is "on camera." They'll even wait to have a shocked or amazed reaction.

If you slow down the footage frame-by-frame, you can often see them glance at the camera; it only lasts a microsecond and is barely perceptible, but they are making sure the camera is on them getting the right shot.

Shooters are naturally drawn to these people because they're so easy to work with. It's a skill that celebrities develop -- someone famous always knows when there's a camera on them, and they know how to work that camera.

The crew should neither encourage nor discourage this skill. Just be aware of the phenomenon. You may think you're playing with them -- but they're playing with YOU.

Over time, everyone else in the show will develop these skills as well. At first, people may avoid the cameras. Others may even try to keep them away. But the camera crews will just work doubly hard to keep up with them.

Soon they'll realize that it's all too much work. It's easier to just let the cameraperson shoot the scene. It's easier to slow down as they walk to the bar instead of speeding up. They'll get to know the crews and realize they're regular people like everyone else, and they'll let them do their jobs.

They'll adjust in small ways. They'll move over on their bed to let the shooter get a better angle. They'll cross the room to talk to someone instead of talking from ten feet away -- because it's easier for both the crew and for them.

This happens naturally. You don't want to force it. The shooters will be silently encouraging it anyway. If one cast member always makes it tough for the camera, the shooter's body language will show his frustration. He may sigh. He may even drop his camera away from his eye, look at the cast member and shrug.

The shooter isn't directing the cast member or telling him to alter his behavior in any way. The shooter is silently saying, "I'm here every night and I always get the same shots from the same spots. Please, let me do my job." The cast member will adapt, especially if you've done your job and everyone's getting along.

Again, no words need ever be exchanged. And although it's not as "real" as it would have been if there were no cameras around, everyone's reactions and behaviors are still honest.

INTERVIEWS

On reality TV shows you generally interview each cast member once a week for about an hour.

Any longer than an hour and their energy level goes down. If you wait longer than a week between interviews, there's a chance that the cast members will forget what happened to them or no longer care and they won't recall what happened to them with enough passion.

By interviewing them each once a week, you also keep their role in the show in the front of their minds. They remember what you talked about and they incorporate the important issues into their lives.

Let's break down the job of an interviewer. This is crucial because the interviews fill out the stories and help drive the stories.

First, an interviewer must act as a:

I - REPORTER

These shows have no narration. Anything that happens in the show that's not clear must be explained in interview. This is the "who what where why and how" of basic reporting.

"Who is your roommate?" "Where is the house exactly?" "How long does it take to get from A to B?" It has nothing to do with emotion and everything about letting the audience know what's going on.

"The weekend trip was to Mt. Hood, which is in Oregon, so it took about twelve hours to get there. Then it started raining."

The cast member is just giving you facts: this is what happened to me this week. But it's this narration which tells us what's going on so you can tell the rest of the story.

Each cast member will have their own "facts" which they need to report each week, and you must get all their facts in short concise sentences.

Be careful -- for the overall group facts you don't need to ask the same questions of everyone. Once you have one good answer about the trip to Mt. Hood, you probably don't need to ask another.

Find your story-teller. Look for a cast member to be your "story-teller." That's the cast member who is generally well-balanced and happy, and isn't necessarily involved in every drama in the cabin.

He may never get a whole episode devoted to him, but he has some distance from the conflicts and is a good observer. Hopefully he is articulate and can give you the big picture. Editors love the character who can sum up the facts of some conflict in a short reasonable soundbite.

You may want to have more than one storyteller in your show. It's a skill you can encourage and develop. But make sure you have at least ONE.

II – NOVELIST

Besides basic reporting, you want to get stories. Stories have beginnings, middles, and ends. You must ask questions that lead the cast members to divide their lives...into beginnings, middles and ends.

You must help them recognize the "stories" within themselves. Every cast member has a drama worthy of a novel.

Bob may be in love with Joan. Help him recognize that this is a dilemma. What is the challenge? What is he going to do about it? How does he feel?

This is the interior monologue of the character that can be running as a voice-over -- and it works to make any shot you see of that character more interesting. Bob isn't just lying on his bed resting, staring at the ceiling...he's also deep in love with Joan.

You're not telling him to do something about Joan, you're asking him to recognize the conflict. You ask him if he has any plans. You ask him if he's thought about it.

If he says, "no," you can say "I'll let you think about that and ask you that question again next time."

The next time he is alone in the room with Joan and you show up with a camera, I guarantee he'll be thinking about his "dilemma."

Whatever roller coaster ride Bob and Joan go on, you must be able to ask them the questions that will force them to track their progress. Encourage them to find a resolution: it could be sad understanding, happy friendship, or hot steamy love.

But get one of them eventually to say, "that's it, story's over, this is how it's going to be."

And you say to yourself, "for now..."

III – FILMMAKER

The cast members' interior monologue that you seek as a novelist only goes so far. This is still a visual medium and you need pictures to go with all the cast members' interior conflicts.

What physical activities are they doing? Do any of them act as metaphors for what they are trying to accomplish as people?

Let's say there's a cast member who is a loner who loves to exercise. Shooting him exercising by himself creates a metaphor...he's creating the body armor he needs to keep people away. He is muscular and scary on the outside, but doesn't let people inside. You now have a physical activity to match his interior mind-set.

As you know people's habits you will see opportunities arise. The Story Department thinks this way, and will be your ally.

IV - BAD THERAPIST

You will sometimes feel like a therapist...a bad therapist.

At first, the cast members might think the interview is a chance to "rap" for an hour, to download their thoughts for the week. It's okay for them to feel that way, but that's not the point of the interview. It's work, and part of their job as cast members.

They may drift on, chatting about some story they want to tell you, but you must find a gentle way to nip their musings in the bud and steer it back to getting the soundbites you need for your TV show.

If the cast members respect and like you, they will also ask you what you think about their problems. But your job isn't to help solve their problems.

Your main job is to say, "I don't know...what do you think about that?" You want their responses for a TV show.

You don't want to be their friend, nor their therapist. You can enjoy their company and like them as people, but ultimately, they are colleagues in the TV show you are all making together.

This doesn't mean you can't have real conversations. That is crucial. You want to build trust and you want them to succeed. But you don't want to go beyond that.

Remember that anything you say about yourself may end up in a scene. You're fascinating to them and if they know something about you, you'll suddenly hear them bring it up in the middle of a conversation. You're not what the show is about.

Maintaining that distance is very important, and crossing the line during production creates confusion that takes energy away from the cameras.

V – FARMER

You want to plant seeds. If you don't keep your cast members thinking about what you need for the next "act" of your story, they'll forget about it.

Ask questions that make people consider what they should do next. Ask questions that gently nudge the cast members into moving their stories forward.

The answer they give in interview might be horrible and not serve the editor at all, but you're not asking these questions for the editor. These questions serve you, the director, because they make the cast member think. They nudge him to keep moving down a particular story line.

Some people want to avoid conflict and drama, even to the point of refusing to think about it. Again, you are not telling them what to say, do, or think. But asking these questions will keep their issues fresh in their minds.

INTERVIEW "TRICKS"

Is an interview a conversation? An interrogation? Is it a scene you need to direct, like in a movie? Yes, it's all these things, and more.

Anything you do that gives you "soundbites" that you can use is legal.

WARM-UPS AND IDs

Have them say who they are (first names only), and their age at the start of every interview. You may want to throw in where they are from. Have them do it several times.

This does three things. First, it warms up the interview subject. This is a comforting ritual that starts off every interview. Second, it immediately identifies who is speaking for the transcriber back in Los Angeles.

Third, it gets them comfortable with performing to the camera. By the fourth interview, they'll be looking right into the lens like a TV talk show host, saying " I'm Bob, I'm 26, and I'm from Seattle."

This is important, because the first time WE EVER SEE THEM ON SCREEN IN THE FIRST EPISODE will be with one of these "into the lens" identifications. You want them to appear casual. If you wait until the last week to do your IDs, then they'll understand that this "new thing" is somehow different and just for the TV show, and it's a performance. You'll end up asking them to "act natural."

Then have a couple of questions that mean nothing to start off the interview...just easy idle chit-chat.

Get people to use your question in your answer, to use people's first names, and to speak in the "present tense."

This isn't easy to do. If the interview is flowing like a conversation, the person wants to say, "It was great! Yeah, I had fun!"

But you can't use that. You have to get them to say, "Hiking up Mt. Hood with Joan was fun." Otherwise, the sentence can't be used for the hiking scene.

Interrupt them right away and get them to start the sentence over. Yes, it will interrupt their emotional flow. But they must specifically identify what and who they are talking about.

If the sentences all have "it was," and "he was," it can't be used, no matter how emotional. And if you get them to say it again, it won't be as powerful and the interview will be twice as long.

They will get used to this. Keep on them and they'll get good at it. Their interviews will go faster.

It's part of their job of being on the TV show. In the same way they must learn how to remove a lavalier microphone without destroying it, they must learn how to speak in full active sentences without pronouns.

Reality TV shows also use the present tense. They should say, "hiking up the mountain is fun..." and not "hiking up the mountain was fun."

People get used to this, and it helps put them back in the moment. It seems odd when you watch the interview, but when it is cut into the final show it adds immediacy.

Avoid yes or no questions.

Their response can only be either yes, or no. You want them to tell you stories and GIVE YOU SOUNDBITES YOU CAN USE.

People downplay their lives. "Up-play" them!

It's very typical for someone to say. "Things are generally good in the house, we are all really getting along, except for Joan, who I have worries about."

The first part of the sentence is an excuse and an apology. The person is somehow embarrassed. The truth is, Joan isn't getting along and Bob's worried! That's the drama.

Get the person to say the second part without the first! After all, it's what they really want to say...the first part is just a caveat. Draw it out of them, get them to say what it is they mean, without excuses.

That also helps them to recognize the drama within their own lives keep the story going.

A month later, the same person might say, "things aren't perfect, there's still a long way to go, but Joan seems to finally be fitting in, so I guess the problem wasn't that bad in the first place."

No! Joan has done hard work to fit in with the group and she is proud of her accomplishment! So are you, that's why you're saying it! There's no shame in being proud! You've arrived somewhere! Enjoy it!

If anything, you must work to get them to recognize other people's points of view. They may hate another cast member and have no qualms about saying it. That's good drama, but to keep the drama going that person may need to change. You may need to ask them to consider how the other person feels.

Get them to use active verbs, story-telling verbs.

"My goal for the weekend is..."

"My greatest challenge on this boat is..."

"I knew I was facing my greatest fear when..."

"I changed the most when..."

"Losing the mission was a big set-back for me...

"The lesson I learned was..."

If you ask questions with interesting and active verbs, the cat members will use them too. They will use the words and help put their experiences into either a first, second, or third act for you.

Every story is about change. You must find the verbs that fit into each act of the story you're telling. Get them to talk about how they feel and think, and get them to use those verbs.

Have a conversation. Argue. Stumble.

You may know everything that's going on with a cast member -- but you want them to tell it to *you*.

They may not want to talk about it. If you stumble and seem confused about what's going on, they may want to clear it up.

"Can you help me make sense of all this? I'm confused..."

Lure it out. He might give you one-word answers, but he does admit he likes Joan. Then, it's completely fair to ask him -- "Can you tell me that in a whole sentence?"

Use Contradiction.

Some people give their best answers when they're defending themselves or contradicting something you said.

Example:

Q: "What do you think of the food on this cruise ship?"

A: "The food is okay I guess."

This answer is lukewarm.

Second example:

Q: "In the dining hall, you go for seconds. Here's your chance to tell us how much you love the food here."

A: Are you kidding me? The food here is terrible, I hate it! You wouldn't catch me going for seconds in a million years!

This is a better answer.

Give them time to think about the overall big questions:

Q: Why don't relationships work out these days?

Q: What is it that women(men) just don't understand about the opposite sex?

These are bigger questions, conceptual questions. Give them time to answer these questions. Come back to them in different interviews.

Get them to talk about each other!

People don't like to talk about themselves, and they don't like to admit to their mistakes or shortcomings...even if you have plans to redeem them by Act Three.

But people always love to share their opinions about the folks around them -- who they are, their struggles, how far they have to go, how they've changed, and what they need to do.

So remember to ask the cast members about each other. It reinforces that this is a show about relationships.

This is the perhaps the most important overall note for a reality TV show.

When you have a storyline developing about a cast member that you know will end up in a show, the finished episode will have more soundbites coming from the people around him than that actual cast member.

The story may mostly show that cast member-- but most of the interviews will probably be other people.

It's about the soundbite!

You will hear lines come out...and you'll know when you hear it -- "that's going to be in the show." That's the feeling you want.

You are always looking for the one great line. Learn to recognize it, and when you hear it, pause and let it hang there. Don't rush to the next question.

The music will swell and the editor will hold that shot for two full seconds. It can be powerful.

On-The-Fly Interviews

On-the-fly interviews work great when a cast member is in the middle of doing something.

"How does it feel watching the other people bungee-jump knowing your turn is coming up?"

This is a typical OTF question that works great. You enter the cast member's mind at that moment, you feel their fear, and the background makes sense with what the cast member is saying.

But an OTF question stops working if the question is not part of the action taking place.

"You've complained that you feel outside the group -- is the bungee jumping somehow bringing you all together?"

This question is still in the moment, but it's now entering the cerebral. As long as the cast member keeps talking about himself and bungee jumping, you're fine. But if they start talking about group dynamics, you're now entering dangerous territory.

"How do you think Bobby is fitting into the group?"

This is definitely a dangerous OTF question, because the look of the shot (a bungee-jumping platform) jars with the answer.

This may not seem this way in the field, but remember, the editor has dozens of interviews to choose from.

When the cast members talk about general group struggles or about each other, the editor's best choices are in the traditional interview set-up.

When you cut in a non-specific OTF with these well-designed interview shots, the OTF stands out as being different and therefore jarring...no matter how interesting and thoughtful the answer is.

By the second round of notes, the question has generally been asked again in interview and the jarring OTF shot has been replaced.

But what if you have to get it now?

Sometimes a cast member has the flu, is frustrated, or is ecstatic about something. If you wait until the Saturday interview the emotion of the moment may have passed.

This OTF can be great as long as the cast member is talking about himself at that moment.

But be careful -- if the cast member starts talking about the other cast members or about "bigger questions" then the OTF and the answer probably won't get used.

What NOT to do:

Don't antagonize or humiliate or confront them. Don't force them to do anything. Don't force them to say anything.

If you surprise them with information that you know that they don't, they will lose trust in you.

You can push the edges, but you risk losing a cast member. After one painful interview, that cast member may mentally check out of the show and just hang around for the ride.

STORIES YOU'LL ENCOUNTER

Trips: Trips are great because they have a built-in story structure that's easy to follow. The cast members sit down and plan a trip. They head out to their destination. They achieve their goal. They come back. It's the easiest story to understand and to cover.

If everyone is prepared, the times that the story beats will occur are even written down on the schedule. Everyone on the crew can read and recognize the crucial story elements ahead of time.

The challenge with trips is to try to figure out which part of the trip is actually the story.

"Voyage" stories are either about the trip there, the time spent there, or the trip back. The other parts of the journey are always much shorter in comparison.

The story department and the editor will always choose one leg of the voyage. The rest will be chopped down to close to nothing.

You can save time and energy if you can judge this as you go. Which leg of journey is the important one?

If the important part is still yet to come, don't kill yourself on the way there, or you won't have enough energy left to get the real story. If you've got your story already, relax and think about what few shots you need for the shorter leg of the journey.

This doesn't mean you shouldn't be attentive and ready in case something happens. It just means be realistic. Most of the trip will be hacked away in the edit bay anyway.

Also, be aware that trips are repetitive motion. A hike on TV consists of a shot of a foot on a rock, a foot on another rock, passing a tree, and heading up the mountain. The shots near the bottom of the mountain look about the same as the ones near the top.

Figure out how to make the shots more interesting, and hone in on finding the stories within that repetitive motion.

The Shorter Story:

Short stories occur in a very brief amount of time:

An intense mission...a brother visits for the weekend...the first day in the house/cabin/ship.

You also have to figure out what to eliminate as you're doing it. Many reality TV missions are designed to give the crew more than they need...which means you can't possibly shoot it all.

Keeping that in mind, focus in fast on what works, and which cast members are giving you the best stories. If you try to cover everything, you may not get enough substantial scenes or moments.

You also must get everyone's reactions during the event in OTFs, or shortly after it happens. If you interview the best alligator wrestler two weeks after his big win, there's less excitement.

The good thing about "short stories" is they are over quickly and you know whether you got the story or not.

The Longer Story:

The long form story may take all season to tell. They include:

How one cast member changed from the first day to the last. Homesickness. The long slow flirtation that leads to romance. Friendship. The challenges of being young in the modern world. Learning to get along as a group.

Some of the stories may be more conceptual, and don't have any solid scenes built-in. If you're gathering material for the alligator wrestling mission, you know what to shoot. If you're gathering material for a story about the difference between men and women, who is the "Candy Man" at camp, scenes from any part of the eight-week shoot schedule could fall under this umbrella.

You have more time to gather the material for these stories, but they can also drift away and disappear. You can keep them alive in interview for a while, but if the cast members don't deliver any scenes with visuals, then the story dies.

You must keep tracking these bigger thematic stories, trying to keep them alive, while also looking for new stories on the horizon.

One nice thing about the long form story is that lots of different kinds of shots work.

If the story is about Bob's deep crush on Joan, most of the story takes place in his head. Shots of Bob staring out the window, walking by himself, smiling at Joan, watching the sunset, even brushing his teeth, can be used to "dramatize" his dilemma. Of course, Bob may not have been thinking about his crush on Joan while any of these shots were being done...but the editor uses them to tell the story.

The Cast Members as "Characters"

If you put any seven people in a room for long enough, something begins to happen. Characters emerge.

Someone will emerge as the joker. Someone else may insist on being a leader. Someone else might be a rebel. Someone else might be the quiet one. Someone else may be a "fish-out-of-water" who never adjusts. Someone else may always be concerned with communicating, building bridges so everyone gets along.

What's fascinating is that the same characters tend to emerge over and over again.

It happens whenever people are thrown together. Sometimes one person will carry two character roles.

Reality TV does not cast for these "types." Reality TV casts first and foremost for interesting people who the audience will love to watch. But the casting department is aware of what each person may bring to the group.

Sometimes a cast member who is a "comedian" at home will arrive on the show and discover he's not the funny guy after all -- someone else has his role. He has to settle for "quiet guy," or "peace-maker."

There have been enough reality shows on TV now that when people apply to be on a show they sometimes have an idea in their head which former cast member they'll most be like. They sometimes even talk about it in the footage.

This is a testament to how these reality shows have become a part of pop culture. A generation ago kids argued about which Brady Bunch kid they were most like. Now they argue about which Real World cast members they're most like.

But this can be irritating for the crew. We want people to just be themselves, and not carry around pop culture baggage. The best cast members are those people who are just themselves who don't worry about which character they are.

Besides, these character types by themselves are interesting only to a point.

What's more interesting is the individual behind the role. Who is more than he or she appears to be? Who starts out in one role and ends up in another? Who sheds their "type" completely and becomes an individual, unique to themselves?

What's also interesting is the dynamic between the different character types.

Who ends up becoming friends despite their seemingly opposite roles? Who is the unlikely leader? These suddenly emerge as good stories.

Reality TV makes shows for a younger audience. And when you are in your teens and twenties you are exploring who you are. That includes sex, clothes, hair styles, sub-cultures. Everyone's trying out new identities.

Use these character roles to make your stories stronger. If there's one cast member who's the tough guy, then try to get shots of him being strong and assertive. That's your starting point. Then watch and wait for him to change into something else...maybe Mr. Sensitivity. That becomes your story.

FINAL NOTE: IS IT REAL?

A reality show is not a traditional documentary. In a traditional documentary you track real people in their own environments.

Reality TV takes real people and puts them in a different environment than their own -- a house, a Winnebago, or a Cruise ship. The environment has been constructed, but the behavior within the environment is real.

This creates a show different than fictional shows and different than traditional documentaries.

For the first four seasons one of the symbols of the Real World was a fish tank, full of exotic fish. Would those fish ever normally share the same space and food out in the wild? No. Within that environment, were they behaving like real fish? Yes. It's an apt metaphor for the experience of the show itself.

You are not creating false situations. You are not fabricating reality. There is nothing fake or contrived about what you are doing and the results you get.

Traditional documentaries in some sense are MORE contrived. They stage shots, like "walk and talks." The documentary subject knows when the cameras will arrive and can prepare ahead of time. None of that happens on a reality TV show. It's 24/7.

People will still make their own decisions, and having honest reactions. You just happen to be participating.

Would their reactions be different and more "real" if you weren't participating? Maybe. And they'd even be more "real" if the cast members had no TV cameras around. By putting them in a TV show you have changed their lives already. But within that context, you can participate, have fun, and keep it real.

Just remember -- so far, the longest finished season of a reality TV show is 24 hour-long episodes -- which can fit on a few DVDs.

So, think about the story and shoot less!

ABOUT THE AUTHOR

Donald Ian Bull has produced, directed and edited many reality TV shows over the past twenty years, including *The Real World, Road Rules, Bug Juice, Camp Jim, Wild Things, The Osbournes, Dr.90210, Beverly Hills Nannies, Project Runway* and more.

He is also a thriller novelist, writing under the name Ian Bull. He is the author of *Liars in Love*, and *Reality Roadkill (A Love Story),* and the thriller series *The Quintana Adventures,* which includes *The Picture Kills* and *Six Passengers, Five Parachutes*. The third book, *Danger Room,* will be out soon.

He also writes essays, including: *CaliforniaBull*, and *Water Markers: Essays on Swimming.*

Please write a review of this book! It will help me reach more readers! Email me at:

IanBullauthor@gmail.com

and I'll show you how.

You can find more writing and free downloads at:

IanBullAuthor.com

28590528R00076